GU01238144

Original title:
A Starry Chill

Author: Kätriin Kaldaru
ISBN HARDBACK: 978-9916-79-555-2
ISBN PAPERBACK: 978-9916-79-556-9
ISBN EBOOK: 978-9916-79-557-6

Cosmic Embrace of the Frost

In the stillness of the night,
The frost begins to gleam,
A blanket soft and white,
It cradles every dream.

Stars shimmer with a glow,
As whispers fill the air,
Each flake a tale to show,
Of beauty pure and rare.

Moonlight dances on the snow,
Painting scenes of wonder,
In this cosmic glow,
Hearts ignite like thunder.

Beneath the vast expanse,
We find our place in time,
In winter's quiet trance,
Love's echo starts to chime.

Together we will soar,
In this frosty embrace,
Through the celestial door,
We find our sacred space.

Icy Whispers of Celestial Beauty

Underneath the silver skies,
The world is ever bright,
Icy whispers softly rise,
In the canvas of the night.

Every flake a secret lost,
Carved by time and grace,
In this chill, we bear the cost,
Of beauty we embrace.

Trees adorned with crystal lace,
Bathed in gentle light,
Nature holds a sacred space,
Filling hearts with delight.

Snowflakes drift like tender sighs,
In their silent flight,
Carrying all of our ties,
To the vast, starry night.

As we wander hand in hand,
Through this frozen scene,
Love is our guiding strand,
In a world so serene.

Starlit Winter's Kiss

Underneath the starlit sky,
Winter blankets all,
Whispers of a lullaby,
On the earth, they fall.

Sparkling in the moon's embrace,
Every path aglow,
Time unfolds with gentle grace,
As the cold winds blow.

In the hush of frosty air,
Magic weaves its thread,
Love's warmth is everywhere,
In the silence spread.

Moments freeze in starlight's kiss,
Holding dreams so tight,
In this ethereal bliss,
We dance through the night.

Together, we shall roam,
In this winter's white,
Finding in the universe,
A love, pure and bright.

Silent Radiance

In the hush of night, a glow,
Soft whispers of stars on snow.
A gentle light, serene and pure,
In silence, our hearts find the cure.

Moonbeams dance on the still ground,
In their embrace, peace is found.
Each twinkle tells a silent tale,
Of dreams that linger, soft and pale.

The world holds its breath in grace,
As night weaves its tender lace.
Shadows blend with dreams so bright,
In the arms of the quiet night.

Within the calm, our spirits soar,
Chasing echoes, forevermore.
The silent radiance guides our way,
Through twilight's soft, ethereal play.

In stillness, we find our light,
As the stars fill the velvet night.
A dance of hope, a sweet refrain,
In silent radiance, we remain.

Midnight's Frozen Caress

Underneath the midnight sky,
Whispers cold, a soft goodbye.
A breath held in the crisp night air,
Frozen moments, sweet and rare.

Stars like diamonds in the gloom,
Illuminate the darkened room.
Each glimmer, a fleeting kiss,
In the night, a world of bliss.

Shadows curl around the trees,
Caressed by a gentle breeze.
The silence sings a haunting song,
In its depth, we all belong.

A frozen touch upon the face,
Time stands still in this embrace.
Each heartbeat echoes loud and clear,
In midnight's arms, we shed our fear.

Wrapped in warmth of winter's spell,
In this stillness, all is well.
Midnight's caress, so cold yet fair,
A dance of dreams that fill the air.

Dreams Wrapped in Silver

In the twilight, shadows play,
Dreams wrapped in silver drift away.
Like whispers on the edge of night,
They dance beneath the pale moonlight.

Softly woven, visions gleam,
In the quiet, we dare to dream.
Each thought a thread of shining lace,
In the realm of time and space.

Underneath the silver sky,
Wishes float and gently sigh.
With every heartbeat, hopes arise,
In this world where magic lies.

Let the dreams take flight and soar,
As silver wings open the door.
To realms where wishes find their way,
In shimmering hues of soft array.

Awash in light, we find our place,
Embracing joy in each embrace.
Wrapped in silver, boundless and free,
In the heart's deep, lasting sea.

Chill of the Constellation

In the night, the stars align,
Whispers chill like ancient wine.
A tapestry of light and dark,
The universe ignites a spark.

Beneath the vast and endless sky,
Galaxies twinkle, drift, and sigh.
In the chill, a cosmic dance,
Every moment, a fleeting chance.

The mysteries of time unfold,
In constellations, tales retold.
Every heartbeat shares a truth,
In the quiet, we find our youth.

Among the stars, dreams take flight,
As shadows fade into the light.
The chill wraps us in its embrace,
In the vastness, we find our place.

Let the chill of night inspire,
A spark of hope, a growing fire.
In the cosmos, both vast and near,
We dance with stars, losing all fear.

Frozen Lullabies

In the quiet of the night,
Whispers soft, pure delight.
Snowflakes dance upon the ground,
Silent dreams, a peace profound.

Crystals shimmer in the dark,
Moonlight glows, a gentle spark.
Frosted branches, nature's grace,
Wrapped in warmth, a bright embrace.

Children's laughter fills the air,
In this world, without a care.
Every breath a cloud of white,
Swaying gently, holding tight.

As the stars begin to gleam,
Nighttime wraps us in a dream.
Hearing echoes from afar,
In this stillness, find a star.

Through the shadows, softly glide,
An angel by our side resides.
With each lullaby we sing,
Winter's joy, a blessed thing.

Nightfall's Glimmer

When the sun dips from the sky,
Stars begin their soft reply.
Whispers of the night's embrace,
Glimmers spark through time and space.

Cooler air begins to hum,
Crickets chirp, a low strum.
Dreams awaken, shadows blend,
Nightfall's magic never ends.

In the stillness, hearts unite,
Beneath the cloak of soft twilight.
A thousand wishes find their flight,
Under the vastness, pure delight.

Time stands still, a moment sweet,
As the world begins to sleep.
Wrapped in starlight, we shall stay,
In the glow, we drift away.

Every sigh a lullaby,
As the moon begins to rise.
In the night, dreams intertwine,
In this glimmer, hearts align.

Ethereal Embrace of Twilight

As the sun begins to fade,
Colors dance in dusk's parade.
Draped in hues of softest grace,
Twilight holds a warm embrace.

Gentle breezes brush our skin,
Whispers of where dreams begin.
In the shadows, secrets weave,
In this moment, we believe.

Fragrant flowers close their eyes,
Underneath the velvet skies.
Every cloud a kiss of light,
Painting magic in the night.

As the stars begin to twinkle,
Time in stillness starts to crinkle.
Holding hands beneath the glow,
In twilight's arms, our love will flow.

Through the calm, our spirits rise,
As the world softly sighs.
In this realm where dreams take flight,
We find solace in the night.

Cosmic Breath of Winter

Winter whispers through the trees,
Echoes carried on the breeze.
Stars align in frozen air,
A cosmic dance, beyond compare.

Snowflakes fall like twinkling light,
Covering the world in white.
Each flake tells a tale untold,
Woven dreams of soft and cold.

In the night, silence reigns high,
Underneath the starlit sky.
Time flows gently, like a stream,
Caught in winter's quiet dream.

Eternal beauty, pure and bright,
In the heart of winter's night.
Each breath shared, a bridge we find,
Connecting souls, forever aligned.

Embrace the cosmic lullaby,
Underneath the folding sky.
In the stillness, our hearts roam,
Winter's breath leads us back home.

Twinkling Night's Blueprint

Stars scatter like seeds,
In the vast fabric of night.
Whispers of dreams take flight,
Under the moon's soft light.

Constellations draw maps,
For travelers of the soul.
In the silence, they unroll,
Guiding hearts to their goal.

Echoes of laughter play,
In the cool evening breeze.
Memories start to sway,
As time bends with such ease.

In the night's gentle arms,
Wonders unfold anew.
Magic in all its forms,
Inviting me and you.

Beneath the twinkling sky,
We gather, hand in hand.
Stories that never die,
In this starlit land.

A Frozen Canopy

Ice lends a crystalline touch,
To the branches overhead.
Nature whispers so much,
In silence, softly spread.

Each flake a tiny gem,
Glitters in the daylight.
Underneath this white hem,
The world is pure and bright.

Footsteps crunch on the path,
Echoing through the trees.
In winter's quiet wrath,
Time pauses with a freeze.

A blanket of silence wraps,
The forest in its hold.
Where unity overlaps,
With stories yet untold.

Underneath the sky's dome,
Nature finds its own voice.
In this frozen home,
The heart learns to rejoice.

Subtle Warmth of Chill

Biting winds carve the air,
Yet comfort starts to bloom.
In the cool, gentle stare,
Beneath winter's cold gloom.

The fire softly crackles,
Drawing friends near and close.
As warm laughter tackles,
The chill's harsh, icy prose.

Scarves wrapped snugly around,
Fingers brushing with care.
Such tenderness is found,
In the crisp evening air.

Hot cocoa in our hands,
Melting away the freeze.
Together, our love stands,
With warmth that always sees.

Chill breezes may blow hard,
But hearts remain aglow.
In life's sweet disregard,
Together, we still grow.

Lullaby of the Frozen Sky

The stars hum a soft tune,
In the cradle of the night.
A lullaby from the moon,
Wrapping all in pure light.

Snowflakes dance in the air,
Falling gentle and slow.
Nature sings with such care,
In winter's sweet tableau.

Each breath a foggy plume,
In the stillness around.
A moment to assume,
In silence profound.

Blankets of white embrace,
The world, so soft and kind.
In this tranquil space,
Peace is what we find.

So let the night be still,
As dreams begin to rise.
In the heart, there's a thrill,
While stars light up the skies.

Frosted Pathways of the Cosmos

Amidst the starlit skies, we tread,
On pathways made of silver thread.
Each breath is crisp, each step a song,
In cosmic realms where dreams belong.

Whispers of the universe call,
As icy echoes gently fall.
With every glance, a world unfolds,
In frozen wonders, stories told.

Through nebulas of glistening frost,
We wander pathways, never lost.
Celestial lights in the dark night,
Guide us softly with their light.

A tapestry of time and space,
Where galaxies in silence trace.
With hearts aglow, we move as one,
In this vast dance beneath the sun.

Each spark a wish, a fleeting thought,
In frosted realms where truths are sought.
A journey fresh, a tale anew,
In cosmic fields of endless blue.

Frozen Echoes Through the Night

The moon hangs high with silver glow,
As frozen echoes start to flow.
They weave through shadows, soft and light,
On nights embraced by frosty bite.

Whispers of the stars take flight,
Painting dreams in shades of white.
Every corner holds a tune,
Underneath the watchful moon.

Chill of winter, crisp and bright,
Dances with the fading light.
Silent moments fill the air,
A world transformed, a dream laid bare.

In this stillness, time stands still,
As frozen hearts begin to fill.
With echoes soft, a voice so clear,
Calling us to draw near.

Through winter's breath, we find our place,
In frozen beauty, a warm embrace.
Together we serenade the night,
With frozen echoes, pure delight.

Night's Icy Mosaic

A canvas vast, of darkness spun,
With icy shards that gleam and run.
Each piece a story, unique and bold,
In night's embrace, a beauty untold.

The stars connect like jewels bright,
In patterns woven through the night.
An endless dance of shadows play,
In night's mosaic, soft decay.

Mirrored dreams in frozen air,
Reflecting whispers everywhere.
Time drips slow, as we observe,
The artistry that night reserves.

Through chilling winds, the tales will blow,
Among the branches wrapped in snow.
A quiet symphony unfolds,
As night reveals what darkness holds.

Within this tapestry of light,
We find our way through endless night.
Each icy piece, a heart that beats,
In night's mosaic, love repeats.

Shimmering Starlit Path

A shimmering path of starlit dreams,
Where hope and wonder softly gleams.
Each step ignites a spark divine,
On trails aglow, our spirits shine.

Through velvet skies, we wander wide,
With twinkling lights that guide our stride.
The universe wraps us in its grace,
As we meander through time and space.

In every star, a wish takes flight,
In every heart, a flame burns bright.
Together we forge this radiant way,
With stardust whispers, come what may.

The night unfolds, a sacred script,
As constellations gently crypt.
Each luminous dot, a tale to tell,
On shimmering paths where shadows dwell.

With eyes uplifted, dreams align,
In starlit realms, our souls entwine.
Through endless night, we'll leave our mark,
On shimmering paths that light the dark.

When Nightfall Embraces

The sky ignites with fading light,
Stars awaken, dreams take flight.
In shadows deep, the secrets lie,
Beneath the vast, unending sky.

Whispers linger, soft and low,
Guiding hearts where moonlight flows.
Candle flames flicker, shadows dance,
In night's embrace, we find our chance.

The world slows down, a gentle hush,
In twilight's glow, we softly blush.
With each breath, the night unfolds,
A tapestry of stories told.

Time drifts on in silver beams,
Wrapped in warmth, we chase our dreams.
With every glance, a spark ignites,
When nightfall calls, we find our sights.

So let us wander, hand in hand,
Through starry realms that gleam and stand.
With night as our companion kind,
In the quiet, we're intertwined.

Ethereal Frost

Whispers of winter, soft and light,
Drape the earth in silver white.
Each breath visible, a ghostly plea,
Ethereal frost, where hearts roam free.

Branches shimmer with icy lace,
Nature dons a chilling grace.
Footsteps crunch on frozen ground,
In every echo, peace is found.

Moonlit nights, so calm and still,
A world transformed by winter's chill.
Stars twinkle like diamonds bright,
In the embrace of velvet night.

Dreams take flight on frosty air,
In this silence, we find care.
The world is wrapped in tranquil dreams,
Where nothing is as it seems.

Time unravels in winter's glow,
Through this beauty, our spirits flow.
Ethereal frost, a fleeting spell,
In its presence, we dwell well.

Illuminated Whispers

Beneath the moon's enchanting light,
Secrets weave through the still night.
Voices soft, like gentle streams,
In illuminated whispers, we dream.

The stars align in cosmic dance,
Every twinkle holds a chance.
Hearts ignite with tales untold,
In the glow, our spirits bold.

Laughter echoes on the breeze,
Carried softly through the trees.
Moments shared, a soulful sigh,
In the warmth, we learn to fly.

Shadows play a timeless game,
In the dark, we learn our names.
With every whisper, souls connect,
In this night, we reflect and respect.

Together, let us find our way,
In the twilight, where shadows sway.
Illuminated whispers guide our flight,
As dawn approaches, we say goodnight.

Cosmic Winter's Embrace

Drifting softly through cosmic night,
Stars unveil their shimmering light.
Galaxies dance in frozen air,
Cosmic winter, a beauty rare.

Snowflakes fall like dreams set free,
Each one unique, a mystery.
A tapestry of time and space,
In this silence, find our grace.

The universe stretches wide and far,
Each breath taken is a stellar star.
In the chill, our spirits soar,
With every heartbeat, we explore.

Boundless skies in midnight hues,
Holding tales in endless views.
In this embrace, we learn to be,
One with the cosmos, wild and free.

So let us wander, hand in hand,
Across the stars, we'll make our stand.
In cosmic winter's gentle clasp,
Eternal wonders, ours to grasp.

Frost-Streaked Reverie

In the morning's gentle light,
Frost paints the world in white.
Dreams whisper on the breeze,
Nature hums with quiet ease.

Crystals dance on leaves aglow,
A shimmering, silent show.
Each breath clouds the chilly air,
Magic hangs everywhere.

Sunrise breaks with golden beams,
Chasing shadows from our dreams.
A world reborn in crystal hue,
Renewal in the morning dew.

Birds take flight with joyous calls,
Frosty layers start to fall.
Life awakens, soft and slow,
In this frost-streaked afterglow.

As daytime fades, the chill appears,
Reminding us of winter's years.
In our hearts, it softly stirs,
A whispered song, the soul's concurs.

Twilight's Frozen Luxury

In twilight's grace, the world unwinds,
Soft hues where day and night entwined.
Stars emerge with silver light,
Draping the land in shimmery night.

Frost-laden branches gently sway,
Cradling secrets of the day.
Whispers float on chilly air,
Magic lingers everywhere.

Moonlit paths, an icy glow,
Adventurers in winter's flow.
A dance of shadows, crisp and clear,
Echoes of dreams that draw us near.

Hearts embrace this frozen charm,
Wrapped in love, a soft, warm balm.
Each moment filled with perfect peace,
As the world holds its breath, we cease.

Embracing night, we find delight,
In frozen luxury, pure and bright.
Together we shall wander far,
Underneath the evening star.

Glacial Lights of the Milky Way

Beneath the arch of endless night,
Stars like diamonds, twinkling bright.
The Milky Way stretches wide,
A glacial stream where dreams reside.

Frozen whispers fill the air,
As constellations dream and flare.
Each flicker holds a tale unknown,
A universe of seeds sown.

Night's embrace is cool and deep,
A cradle where the cosmos sleeps.
Galaxies swim in twilight's grace,
In this vast, celestial space.

Moments linger, time stands still,
Under the sky, we feel the thrill.
Captured in this ethereal play,
Marvel at the glacial display.

With every breath, the magic flows,
Filling hearts as the starlight glows.
Boundless dreams in the night unfurl,
Wrapped in the cosmos, a wondrous swirl.

Night's Sparkling Frost

Night descends with gentle grace,
Frosty crystals lace the space.
Stars emerge, a scattered glow,
Painting shadows with their show.

Chill winds weave through sleepy trees,
Carrying whispers with the breeze.
Every breath a cloud of white,
In the stillness of the night.

Moonlight wraps the world in dreams,
Silver sparkles, soft moonbeams.
Every footstep leaves a trace,
In this frost-kissed, quiet place.

Hearts are warmed by winter's breath,
Finding beauty in the depth.
In the night, we stand awake,
Embracing all the frost can make.

As dawn approaches, we'll stay close,
In the night's enchanting dose.
For in this cold, we find delight,
In the beauty of winter's night.

Icy Breath of Midnight

The night sighs softly, breath so cold,
Whispers of secrets yet untold.
Crystals dance upon the air,
Moonlight weaves its silver hair.

Silent trees in frozen grace,
Shadows flicker, losing trace.
Stars above begin to hum,
In this stillness, hearts succumb.

Footsteps quiet on the snow,
Echos of the past's soft glow.
With each chill, memories freeze,
Caught within the midnight breeze.

Glimmers from the distant sky,
Frosted dreams that twinkle high.
Underneath the watchful moon,
Nature's lullaby a soothing tune.

Wrapped in night's embrace divine,
Time drips slowly, sweetly twine.
In this grasp, we breathe the dawn,
Yet linger where the night has drawn.

Celestial Shadows

Stars descend, casting their veil,
In the dark, where whispers sail.
Celestial shadows dance and play,
Guiding lost souls on their way.

Moonbeams flicker, weaving light,
A gentle touch in the heart of night.
Each twinkle tells a timeless tale,
Of cosmic secrets, bright and pale.

Planets spin in silent grace,
Tracing paths in empty space.
Older than time, their stories told,
In radiant hues of silver and gold.

Eclipsed by dreams, we drift away,
In celestial realms where spirits sway.
Gravity's pull, a sweet embrace,
Within the stars, we find our place.

Hold me close in shadows deep,
Where the universe decides to sleep.
In this night, forever dwell,
In celestial shadows, all is well.

Starlit Frostbite

In the heart of a bitter night,
Stars above, a shimmering sight.
Every breath a misty plume,
Breath of winter, nature's bloom.

Frosty tendrils grasp the ground,
Blanketing all without a sound.
Nights like these, both harsh and sweet,
In silence, hear the winter's heartbeat.

Awake in dreams that shimmer bright,
Starlit paths, guiding the light.
Crystals form on branches bare,
A tapestry of beauty rare.

Cold winds whisper secrets low,
Carrying tales of long ago.
Lost in the dance of winter's thread,
Where icy whispers gently spread.

In starlit frostbite, souls align,
Bound by dreams in the frosty vine.
Through the chill, our spirits rise,
As the night unfolds its skies.

Moonlit Chill

A silver glow, the world is still,
Caught within the moonlit chill.
Glimmers touch the frozen stream,
Wrapped in night's enchanting dream.

Shadows linger, hold their breath,
Chilled by whispers of quiet death.
Underneath the moon's soft gaze,
Life and death in timeless ways.

Branches creak like aged old bones,
Echoes where the stillness moans.
In the night's embrace, we find,
Reflections of a wandering mind.

Frosty air, a lingering kiss,
In this moment, we find bliss.
Stars descend from distant heights,
Embracing all with gentle lights.

Moonlit chill, let shadows play,
In the depth of night, we stay.
Together lost in winter's thrall,
Where the moonlit magic calls.

Icy Fragments of Night

In the silence of the dark,
Shimmers dance like a breeze,
Fragments of ice softly spark,
Whispers float with such ease.

Moonlight weaves through the cold,
Casting glances on the ground,
Stories of night unfold,
In shadows, magic is found.

Crystals hang on the trees,
Glittering like cherished dreams,
Frozen songs in the freeze,
Lullabies that softly gleam.

Through the night, a soft sigh,
As frost kisses every seam,
Underneath the starry sky,
I drift into a sweet dream.

Embrace of the chilling air,
Around, the world holds its breath,
In the icy night so rare,
Life dances with quiet death.

Lattice of Stars and Snow

A lattice of stars above,
Weaves a tale of winter's night,
Glowing softly like a dove,
Bathing earth in purest light.

Snowflakes twirl in gentle flight,
Each a jewel, uniquely spun,
Whispers carried through the night,
Erasing traces of the sun.

In the stillness, dreams arise,
Nature's blanket, pure and white,
Beneath vast, uncharted skies,
Lies a world of pure delight.

Footsteps pressed in crisp, cold ground,
Echo softly, fade away,
In the silence, peace is found,
As the stars begin to play.

Tales untold in flakes of snow,
Link the heavens to the earth,
In this lattice, whispers flow,
Marking winter's gentle birth.

Whispering Lights

Whispering lights in the air,
Dimming gently as they sway,
Trail of colors everywhere,
Painting night, turning it to day.

Across the sky, they twinkle bright,
Stars descend and kiss the stream,
In their glow, the world feels right,
Wrapped in warmth, lost in a dream.

Softly flickering, they dance,
Guiding lost souls on their way,
Giving hope, a fleeting chance,
In the dark, they come to stay.

Embers sparkling in the night,
Glistening like diamonds rare,
Every flicker brings delight,
Whispers linger everywhere.

Through the shadows, secrets find,
Paths illuminated bright,
In the heart, a warmth combined,
With the whispering of lights.

Ethereal Twilight Chill

In the twilight's gentle chill,
Colors melt into the sky,
Where the world stands, softly still,
And day bids its sweet goodbye.

Echoes of the sun retreat,
As shadows extend their hands,
Lands painted with hues so sweet,
In this moment, beauty stands.

A breath of night, a sighing breeze,
Whispers secrets of the dark,
Rustling leaves dance with such ease,
Stirring hearts to leave their mark.

Ethereal glow on the snow,
Softened edges, calm and clear,
In this twilight, dreams will grow,
Embraced by the shadows near.

Underneath the sprawling sky,
A chill wraps around the earth,
In this peace, we wonder why,
It's in twilight we find mirth.

Enigmatic Stars Above

In the dark canvas of night,
Stars shimmer with ancient light.
Whispers of secrets untold,
Their mysteries in silence unfold.

Galaxies swirl in their dance,
Spirits of magic, take a chance.
Guiding lost souls through the haze,
They illuminate the starry blaze.

A tapestry stitched with dreams,
Threads of time in silver beams.
Echoes of worlds from afar,
Reveal the truths, like a star.

In their glow, we find our peace,
Moments of joy that never cease.
Stars above, a silent guide,
In their brilliance, we confide.

Each twinkle holds a wish to share,
Infinite dreams that fill the air.
Enigmatic stars, shining bright,
Forever a beacon in the night.

Winter's Starry Veil

Under winter's blanket of white,
Stars shine with a frosty light.
Whispers of snowflakes in the air,
Gentle beauty, beyond compare.

The nights stretch long and bold,
Stories of warmth through the cold.
In this quiet, we find our song,
As the world sleeps, we belong.

A tapestry of silver threads,
Each one where hope gently spreads.
Mirrored in stillness, hearts take flight,
Carried softly into the night.

Frozen breath in the silent air,
Each moment, a dream laid bare.
Winter's embrace, tender and bright,
A starry veil cloaked in night.

With every twinkle, spirits rise,
Guided by the moonlit skies.
In this winter, feel the charm,
Wrapped in starlight, safe and warm.

A Dance of Frost and Light

In the chill of a moonlit night,
Frost and light begin their flight.
Whispers of elegance abound,
In their waltz, beauty is found.

Icicles glisten, sharp and clear,
Reflecting dreams we hold dear.
With each movement, shadows play,
In this dance, we drift away.

Twinkling gleams on snowy ground,
Echoes of joy, softly profound.
A ballet where silence sings,
Nature wraps us in its wings.

Frosted breaths in the crisp air,
Moments of wonder laid bare.
Through this dance, hearts intertwine,
In the glow where stars align.

Blossoming softly like the dawn,
Embracing the magic, we are drawn.
Frost and light, a timeless rhyme,
In their rhythm, we lose track of time.

Night's Icy Canvas

The night unfurls her icy sheet,
Stars etch dreams with every beat.
Cold whispers weave through the air,
On this canvas, magic's laid bare.

Each constellation tells a tale,
Guiding lost hearts to prevail.
The moon's glow, a gentle touch,
In this stillness, we feel so much.

Snowflakes dance in frosty light,
Creating wonders out of sight.
Layered silence, a soothing balm,
In the chill, we find our calm.

Midnight paints with a silver brush,
Colors of dusk in a quiet hush.
Each twinkle shares a secret thought,
In this realm, we seek what's sought.

A canvas drawn with care and grace,
Each stroke a wish, a warm embrace.
Night's icy wonder whispers sweet,
In the dark, our dreams repeat.

Luminous Cold

In the quiet night, stars glow bright,
Frosty whispers chill the air so light.
Moonbeams glisten on the icy ground,
A shimmering beauty all around.

Trees wear crystals, nature's crown,
In the stillness, shadows drown.
Breath turns to mist, a soft sigh,
Underneath the vast, cold sky.

Echoes of silence, tranquil and deep,
The world shimmers, as if in sleep.
Footsteps crunch on the powdered snow,
A serene peace begins to grow.

Heartbeats resonate with the chill,
Winter's song, a steady thrill.
Each flake dances, unique, divine,
In this luminous cold, we intertwine.

Embrace the frost, let spirits soar,
As nature's beauty opens a door.
In the heart of winter's embrace,
We find warmth in its quiet grace.

Spark of the Icy Skies

Underneath the twinkling night,
Frozen dreams take to flight.
Stars like diamonds sparkle bright,
Guiding souls with gentle light.

The heavens breathe a chilling glow,
Whispers dance on winds that blow.
Each breath is a cloud, pure and white,
A tapestry of beauty, a true sight.

Snowflakes fall, they swirl and spin,
A soft symphony, where dreams begin.
Cold air crackles, electric and free,
A spark ignites in you and me.

Reflections of light on ice so clear,
Moments of magic that draw us near.
In this wintry wonder, hearts ignite,
With the spark of the icy night.

Hold on tight to this fleeting bliss,
Nature's artwork, we can't miss.
In the chilly arms of the serene skies,
We find warmth in each other's eyes.

Winter's Celestial Dance

Beneath the moon's soft tender gaze,
Winter weaves her frozen maze.
Stars twirl in their cosmic gate,
A dance of chill that captivates.

Snowflakes pirouette, quiet grace,
In this wintry, timeless space.
Every flake a story untold,
In the beauty of the winter's cold.

Whispers sound like an old refrain,
Echoes of laughter fall like rain.
Through the trees, a gentle breeze,
Carries dreams with effortless ease.

The world adorned in a frosty trance,
Nature's beauty, a wild romance.
Under stars, we find our chance,
To join in this celestial dance.

Glimmers of silver, pure delight,
As we revel in the winter night.
In the cosmic ballet we find our way,
In winter's embrace, forever we stay.

Illuminated Chill

In the dawning light of a frosty morn,
Nature's palette, crisp and adorned.
Shadows stretch as sun rays break,
A world transformed with every shake.

Each breath of winter, pure and clear,
Carries whispers for us to hear.
A gentle chill wraps 'round us tight,
Illuminated by the soft, warm light.

The shimmer of frost on leaves anew,
Nature's canvas, a stunning view.
Cold winds hum a haunting song,
In this winter, we all belong.

Stars fade slowly in morning's glow,
But memories of night still flow.
Through the frost, the world ignites,
A dance of warmth to chase the nights.

So breathe in deep the winter's thrill,
Embrace the moments, cherish the chill.
In every sparkle, stories lie,
Illuminated chill beneath the sky.

Glittering Shadows

In quiet corners, secrets creep,
Where whispered tales and shadows leap.
A dance of light in dusky air,
Glittering hushed, a hidden flare.

Mysterious forms in twilight's glow,
Softly weaving through the low.
Each flicker tells a story old,
In night's embrace, the dreams unfold.

Characters of darkness play,
Casting spells that lead astray.
Glimmers twinkle, hearts ignite,
In the magic of the night.

Echoes linger, fading fast,
Moments caught in shadows cast.
Through the veil of dusky night,
Glittering worlds, a wondrous sight.

As dawn draws near, the shadows fade,
Yet sweet enchantments are not laid.
In memory's depth, they softly stay,
Glittering whispers, night's ballet.

Beneath the Milky Veil

Stars are draped in a silken shawl,
Whispers of night, a celestial call.
Underneath this vast expanse,
Dreamers gather, lost in trance.

Galaxies twirl in a cosmic waltz,
Each wish cast, an echo, not false.
The universe breathes through the light,
Beneath the veil, the hearts take flight.

Nebulae bloom in colors bright,
Painting the canvas of endless night.
A canvas woven with tales untold,
Hearts beat stronger, hopes unfold.

Echoes of laughter drift through space,
In the quiet, there's a warm embrace.
Together under this stellar dome,
Finding comfort, a place called home.

As dawn approaches, soft and rare,
The Milky Veil begins to glare.
Yet in the light, we hold the thrill,
Of stars that dance and dreams that fill.

The Hush of Winter Skies

Silence blankets the world so wide,
As winter whispers, hearts abide.
Snowflakes fall like gentle dreams,
In frosty air, the stillness beams.

Pines wear cloaks of purest white,
Branches glisten in frosty light.
Each breath forms a crystal glow,
In winter's hush, time moves slow.

Crisp echoes in the frozen air,
Nature beckons with quiet care.
Beneath the stars, the earth sleeps tight,
Wrapped in magic, cloaked in night.

Footsteps softly tread the ground,
In the stillness, peace is found.
Winter's chill, a soothing balm,
In every flake, tranquility's charm.

As the dawn breaks, light draws near,
Winter's hush, now crystal clear.
Yet in this calm, a promise lies,
The warmth will rise, beneath the skies.

Celestial Frostbite

Stars pierce through the midnight chill,
Whispers of frost, a silent thrill.
Each twinkle sparkles, sharp and bright,
In frozen realms where dreams take flight.

The cosmos shivers with icy breath,
Painting the night with whispers of death.
Yet in the cold, the beauty blooms,
In frozen shadows, the magic looms.

Moonlight drapes in silver lace,
Guiding lost souls, a warm embrace.
In the stillness, hearts entwine,
Celestial frost, both cruel and fine.

Glimmers dance on icy streams,
Flowing softly through our dreams.
With every breath, our spirits rise,
Bound together 'neath starlit skies.

As dawn heralds the sun's warm reign,
Frostbite fades, yet leaves a stain.
In memory's grasp, we hold the night,
Celestial wonders, a frost-kissed flight.

Cosmic Frosted Dreams

In the still of night, we gaze up high,
Where dreams are frozen, in the sky.
Stars like whispers, softly gleam,
Carried away in a cosmic dream.

Galaxies swirl in a frosty embrace,
Journeying through this vast, endless space.
Nebulas dance in a celestial waltz,
Painting the void with their silvery squalts.

With every shimmer, a wish takes flight,
Floating through shadows, towards the light.
Cosmic wonders, forever abound,
In the frozen silence, we are spellbound.

In a hush of frost, secrets unfold,
Tales of the universe, patiently told.
Wrapped in starlight, we drift and roam,
In the embrace of the cosmos, we find our home.

As we close our eyes, dreams intertwine,
In the cosmic frost, where hopes align.
With every heartbeat, a promise we keep,
In this celestial frost, we dare to dream deep.

Celestial Crystals in the Dark

In the velvet night, crystals glow,
Scattered like diamonds in a cosmic flow.
They twinkle softly, a guiding spark,
Illuminating paths through the dark.

Each glimmer whispers, ancient lore,
Of shimmering worlds and much more.
Awash in magic, starlit thrill,
With every heartbeat, the universe will.

Dusted in stardust, we dance and sway,
Beneath the crystals, we lose our way.
Galactic treasures in twilight's embrace,
Awakening wonders, in time's gentle pace.

Through the silence, our spirits soar,
With celestial crystals, forever implore.
Navigating dreams where shadows play,
In the warmth of starlight, night turns to day.

In every spark, a story unfolds,
Of beauty and wonder, yet untold.
As we wander forth, our hearts embark,
In the realm of crystals, dancing in the dark.

Frigid Starry Silhouettes

Under the chill of a wintry sky,
Frigid silhouettes quietly fly.
Stars, like sentinels, watch from afar,
Guiding lost souls, as they drift and spar.

In the silence of night, shadows entwine,
Carving their paths, so elegant, fine.
Each flickering flame, a story to tell,
In the icy embrace, where echoes dwell.

With every breath, the cold air sings,
Of distant worlds and celestial things.
Frigid whispers amid the dark air,
In the cosmos' arms, we find our care.

Illuminated dreams, the night unfolds,
A tapestry woven with starlit folds.
In this frosty dance, our spirits ignite,
Painting the heavens with colors so bright.

As silhouettes soar in the cosmic sea,
We find connection, you and me.
In the depths of the void, with hearts that rhyme,
Frigid starry silhouettes transcend time.

Ethereal Chill of the Cosmos

Beneath the moonlight's gentle caress,
The cosmos breathes in soft duress.
An ethereal chill sweeps through the night,
Whispering secrets of endless light.

Stars cascade like whispers untold,
Enchanting the night, a sight to behold.
In this velvet expanse where dreams conform,
The universe dances, alive and warm.

Cradled in silence, the galaxies weave,
Tales of wonder for those who believe.
Through cosmic corridors, shadows might drift,
In the dance of existence, we find our gift.

Ode to the stillness, a celestial hymn,
Where aspirations and realities swim.
In the chill of the cosmos, hearts entwine,
Bound by a force that is tender yet divine.

In this boundless night, our spirits soar,
The ethereal chill invites us to explore.
Each twinkling star, a beacon of hope,
Navigating paths through the galaxy's scope.

Luminous Frost

Upon the glass, a shimmer bright,
The world aglow with winter's light.
Each blade of grass, a crystal's kiss,
In morning's breath, a fleeting bliss.

Beneath the trees, the silence deep,
As snowflakes twirl, the heavens weep.
A tapestry of purest white,
Drapes the earth in soft delight.

Frosted whispers in the air,
Nature's song, a quiet prayer.
With every step, a crunching sound,
In this enchanted world, we're bound.

The moon peeks through the clouds above,
Casting shadows, lighting love.
Fleeting moments, still they last,
In frosty realms, our spirits cast.

As daylight wanes, the colors fade,
Yet in this chill, no fear or shade.
With luminous frost, our hearts aglow,
Together we dance, in winter's show.

Midnight Crystals

Underneath the starlit skies,
Whispers echo, soft and shy.
Midnight crystals sparkle bright,
Glistening gems of pure delight.

Every shadow holds a tale,
In silken threads, the night will veil.
Pale moonlight weaves through the trees,
Carrying secrets on the breeze.

A hush descends, the world at peace,
As dreams unfold and worries cease.
In frozen lands, where silence reigns,
The heart discovers what remains.

Crystal formations, intricate art,
Reflecting the essence of every heart.
As midnight wraps the earth so tight,
We find our way, through endless night.

With each breath, the magic grows,
As winter's beauty softly flows.
In this realm of starry gleam,
We drift away, lost in a dream.

Ethereal Frostflowers

Ethereal shapes on windows bloom,
Delicate patterns dispelling gloom.
Each frostflower, a fleeting sigh,
Wings of winter, bidding goodbye.

Glimmering petals, nature's lace,
In every curve, a gentle grace.
Softly they dance with breath of cold,
Stories of winter, silently told.

As dawn awakens the sleeping dew,
Colors emerge, a vibrant hue.
But in the shadows, they still remain,
Whispers of beauty in winter's reign.

Here lies a world, both fragile and bold,
In these frostflowers, secrets unfold.
A moment captured in time's embrace,
Nature's artistry, a sacred space.

So let us wander through the frost,
In this wonderland, we'll never be lost.
For in each flower, a story grows,
A tapestry of life, the heart knows.

Twilight's Chill

As twilight falls, the air grows still,
A gentle touch, a velvet thrill.
Shadows dance as colors blend,
In the hush, where day must end.

The horizon whispers tales untold,
Of the warmth that day will hold.
Yet in this moment, cool and clear,
We find a peace, so close, so near.

Through fields of blue, the chill does creep,
In starry skies, our dreams shall leap.
A tapestry of dusk unfurls,
As twilight's chill embraces worlds.

Stars awaken, flickering bright,
Guiding us through the enveloping night.
In this balance of dark and light,
We hold each other, hearts taking flight.

In fleeting moments, love shines true,
Echoing softly, me and you.
As twilight fades to midnight's call,
We cherish the beauty, embracing it all.

Echoes of a Frigid Night

Moonlight whispers through the trees,
A chill creeps softly on the breeze.
Footsteps echo, shadows play,
Night unfolds its dark array.

Stars blink down like distant eyes,
Secrets hidden in the skies.
Frosted air, a silver sheet,
Every sound, a heartbeat's heat.

Branches crack with icy breath,
Nature's calm skirts near to death.
A howl breaks the silent hold,
Stories of the night retold.

Softly drifting, the snow falls light,
Wrapping all in purest white.
Underneath, the earth sleeps deep,
In reverie, we quietly keep.

Enchanted moments, shadows blend,
Time suspends, the night won't end.
Echoes linger in this space,
In winter's grasp, we find our place.

Stardust and Snowflakes

Falling gently, the snowflakes twirl,
A dance of dreams in a frozen swirl.
Underneath the cosmic light,
Stardust kisses the winter night.

Whispers of magic fill the air,
Secrets held without a care.
Every flake a story spun,
In the glow of the midnight sun.

Glistening paths where silence reigns,
Nature's blanket, soft refrains.
Each soft landing—a wish made true,
In the stillness, we feel anew.

Stars flicker like a distant flame,
Each one calling out a name.
Underneath this vast expanse,
We find our place within the dance.

So let the world be hushed tonight,
Embracing warmth, igniting light.
In snowflakes' fall, in stars' embrace,
We find our peace in this vast space.

Shimmering Veil of Stillness

A shimmering veil drapes the land,
Silent beauty, softly so grand.
In the hush of evening's breath,
Stillness whispers tales of death.

Glowing softly, the moon ascends,
A guardian where twilight blends.
Stars begin their nightly tune,
Underneath the gentle moon.

Crickets chirp their lullaby,
Nature sings beneath the sky.
A tapestry of quiet grace,
In this tranquil, timeless space.

Embers fade in the fireplace,
Fading light begins to trace.
Shadows dance on walls so bare,
As night unfurls its tender care.

Wrapped in dreams, the world feels right,
Cradled softly by the night.
In the stillness, hearts collide,
Finding solace side by side.

Nocturnal Silk

Nocturnal silk caresses skin,
In darkness, our souls begin.
The night enchants with hidden grace,
Each moment holds a warm embrace.

Stars weave stories high above,
Binding dreams with threads of love.
Underneath the velvet skies,
Whispers echo, softly sighs.

Gentle breezes weave through trees,
Nature's breath, a soothing tease.
As shadows stretch and softly blend,
In twilight's arms, we start to mend.

Footsteps whisper on the grass,
Each heartbeat's rhythm will surpass.
The night reveals its tender face,
In its depths, we find our place.

So let us linger, let us drift,
In dreams that night so freely gifts.
In nocturnal silk, we find our way,
Where hopes ignite and fears decay.

Glimmering Whispers of the Night

Stars dangle softly in the skies,
Whispers of secrets and dreams arise.
Moonlight dances on the tranquil seas,
Carrying tales in a gentle breeze.

Shadows flicker beneath the trees,
Bathed in magic, the world finds peace.
Silent echoes of time long past,
In the night's embrace, we hold them fast.

Crickets serenade with soothing sounds,
Winding paths where wonder abounds.
The air is thick with mystery's thread,
In the stillness where dreams are bred.

Glimmers of hope twinkle in dark,
Each heartbeat ignites a tiny spark.
Lost in thoughts, we drift and sway,
In glimmering whispers, we find our way.

As night deepens, the stars align,
In this moment, your heart meets mine.
Together we weave our dreams so bright,
In the glimmering whispers of the night.

Echoes of the Frosty Cosmos

Through the veil of twilight's embrace,
Echoes of stars, a celestial trace.
Cold winds whisper from galaxies far,
Each twinkle a wish, each breath a star.

Frosty fingers sketch on the glass,
Tales of the cosmos that come to pass.
Crystalline dreams in the frosty air,
Carried away, without a care.

The silence hums with ancient lore,
Of worlds unseen and cosmic shore.
Stardust dances in the moon's glow,
Paths through wonders only few know.

Nebulas bloom in vibrant hues,
As the universe sings its timeless blues.
Each echo ricochets through the night,
A reminder of beauty, fierce and bright.

In the stillness, we catch a glimpse,
Of the vastness that makes hearts wince.
Yet inside this frost, we feel it warm,
Echoes of the cosmos, a protective charm.

Chilling Wonders of the Universe

Cosmic rays brush against the night,
Chilling wonders glow with pure delight.
Galaxies swirl like a painter's dream,
In the silence, we hear the stars' beam.

Planets whisper in the dark void,
Echoes of beauty, never destroyed.
Fading shadows dance, come alive,
In this vastness, our spirits thrive.

Ice crystals form beneath our feet,
Nature speaks softly, oh so sweet.
Wonders abound, secrets to find,
In the cosmos, our hearts unbind.

Nebulous thoughts drift through the air,
As we marvel at the world's affair.
Chilling wonders that never relent,
In the universe's vast adornment.

Stars ignite in eternal flight,
Offering solace, warming the night.
Together we gaze, hand in hand,
In the chilling wonders of this grand land.

Shimmering Nightfall

As dusk descends, the sky ignites,
Shimmering hues, enchanting sights.
Stars awaken, stretching their light,
Bathing the world in soft twilight.

Moonbeams play on the silver streams,
Dancing reflections, weaving dreams.
Whispers of night on a gentle breeze,
Carrying hopes through the swaying trees.

In this hour, magic feels near,
Every shimmer a promise, sincere.
The world transforms in a palette grand,
A canvas painted by nature's hand.

Crickets serenade, the night's delight,
Songs of harmony fill the night.
Lost in moments that softly fall,
Wrapped in the warmth of shimmering call.

As night deepens, we sway and dream,
In shimmering nightfall's tranquil beam.
Hearts entwined under the velvet sky,
In this embrace, together we fly.

A Wisp of Galactic Air

In the silence of the night,
Stars weave a delicate thread,
Whispers of worlds afar,
Glimmers of dreams unsaid.

Nebulas dance in the dark,
Colors that blend and swirl,
In cosmic serenade's spark,
Infinite wonders unfurl.

A sigh from a distant sun,
Breath of the void so vast,
Celestial stories spun,
Echoes of futures passed.

Floating through realms of light,
A voyage on starlit streams,
Carried by hope's delight,
Chasing our wildest dreams.

As the galaxies unfold,
Time bends in cosmic grace,
Secrets of the brave and bold,
In the vastness, we find our place.

The Frosted Horizon's Call

Over hills where silence sleeps,
A whisper rides the icy breeze,
Nature's breath in stillness creeps,
Painting landscapes with its freeze.

The sun breaks through, a golden hue,
Frosted branches glisten bright,
In this moment, pure and true,
Winter's charm is pure delight.

Footprints on the glistening snow,
Stories of journeys made with care,
In the chill, warm hearts will glow,
Wrapped in a cozy layer.

The horizon sings a silent tune,
Calling wanderers from afar,
Beneath the watchful, crescent moon,
Guiding dreams like a twinkling star.

In the quiet of the night,
The frosted world holds secrets tight,
Beneath the winter's crystal veil,
A whisper of magic tells the tale.

Sparkling Wilderness

In the heart of emerald leaves,
Nature's laughter echoes near,
Sunlight dances, softly weaves,
The wilderness, wild and clear.

Streams flow with a crystal sound,
Pebbles glint like polished gems,
In this haven, peace is found,
Among the ferns and wild stems.

Mountains loom with majesty,
Guardians of the earth and sky,
In their shadow, souls are free,
Where the spirit learns to fly.

Wildflowers paint the ground with grace,
Colors burst in vivid sprays,
In this vibrant, open space,
Nature sings in endless ways.

As evening casts a golden glow,
Stars begin their dazzling show,
In the sparkling wilderness bright,
Hearts find joy beneath the night.

Enchanted in the Cold

Beneath a blanket forged in white,
The world transforms, a fairy tale,
Every branch, a pearl of light,
Whispers in the winter's veil.

Crisp air tinged with magic's breath,
Frozen laughter fills the air,
In this place, time pauses, Seth,
Moments linger, light and rare.

Snowflakes dance like fleeting dreams,
Twisting in a chill embrace,
Glowing softly, moonlight beams,
Casting shadows, graceful trace.

As twinkling stars reflect our wishes,
The cold ignites a spark of fire,
In this winter's realm of kisses,
Heartfelt warmth and pure desire.

Enchanted here, in frosty glow,
Lies a love that season's fold,
In the silence, we both know,
Magic blossoms in the cold.

Breath of Celestial Nights

In the vast expanse, dreams take flight,
Whispers of time in the still of night.
Stars gaze down with a tranquil grace,
Guiding lost souls to a sacred place.

Moonbeams dance on the silver sea,
Crickets sing sweetly, their melody free.
A soft breeze carries the scent of pine,
Nature's canvas, a masterpiece divine.

Shadows stretch long, painting the ground,
As the universe spins without a sound.
Moments entwine in the cosmic play,
Ethereal wonders in soft array.

Time seems to pause, a breath held tight,
In the magic that lives under starlit light.
The heart whispers secrets to the dark,
Finding solace in its sacred spark.

Gazing upwards, we lose our fears,
In the tapestry woven of dreams and tears.
A symphony played on the strings of fate,
In the breath of celestial nights, we wait.

Starlit Hush

Under a blanket of velvet skies,
Softly the world in silence lies.
Each twinkle a promise, a story untold,
In the starlit hush, our hearts unfold.

Moonlight glimmers on rivers wide,
Reflecting the dreams that within us bide.
Whispers of love in the night's embrace,
Hold every moment in sacred space.

Crickets serenade with their tender song,
As the night deepens, we drift along.
Hand in hand, we walk this way,
In shadows and light, our fears allay.

Time stands still, in the gentle sway,
Each heartbeat echoes, come what may.
The universe cradles our fleeting sighs,
In the starlit hush, where magic lies.

Lost in wonder, we gaze and dream,
Caught in the web of the silver gleam.
In this quiet dance, we find our place,
In the starlit hush, we embrace grace.

Wistful Flickers in the Cold

In the chill of evening, whispers roam,
Fractured shadows seeking home.
Flickers of warmth like embers glow,
In the depth of winter, love will grow.

Stars shimmer bright in a frosty haze,
Casting soft light on forgotten days.
Nostalgia wraps like a tender quilt,
Woven with dreams and wishes built.

The world stands still, wrapped in white,
Silence dances in the pale moonlight.
Breath of winter, crisp and clear,
Echoes of laughter linger near.

Wistful thoughts drift in the air,
Carried on winds that whisper rare.
Each flicker a moment, a memory bold,
In the tapestry spun of stories told.

Hearts intertwine with the night's embrace,
Finding solace in a shared space.
In the warmth of hope, our spirits unfold,
Amidst the wistful flickers in the cold.

Frozen Reflections Under Stars

Beneath the heavens, the world lies still,
In frozen reflections, we find our thrill.
Mirrors of twilight, a glimmering sheen,
Capture the beauty of moments unseen.

Cold air dances, crisp and bright,
Stars compass our paths in the heart of night.
Each breath a cloud, soft as sighs,
Under the watchful, eternal skies.

Silhouettes whisper secrets of time,
Dreams intertwined as if in rhyme.
Frozen reflections, stories afar,
Each spark a reminder of who we are.

Frost-kissed branches in silver attire,
Glistening softly like celestial fire.
In quiet moments, we linger and pause,
Awed by the universe's silent applause.

With every heartbeat, the night unfolds,
In frozen reflections, our spirits behold.
Together we weave in the starry night,
In the canvas of dreams, we find our light.

Whispers of the Cosmic Breeze

Stars twinkle with secrets rare,
The cosmic winds weave through the air.
Galaxies murmur in silent flight,
Echoes of dreams in the velvet night.

Nebulae dance in hues so bright,
Cradled softly in the arms of light.
Planets whisper tales untold,
Of love and loss, of brave and bold.

Time drifts gently like a feather,
United in this cosmic tether.
Each breath a story, soft and pure,
In this vast expanse, we all endure.

Mysteries swirl in the whispering breeze,
Finding solace amidst the trees.
With every sigh, the universe sings,
A symphony born of celestial things.

In the stillness where wonders gleam,
We find connection within the dream.
The cosmos hums a lullaby true,
In this embrace, just me and you.

Nightfall's Crystal Veil

The sun dips low, a fading ember,
Night cloaks the world, a spell to remember.
In crystal light, the stars align,
Whispering dreams in twilight's sign.

Soft shadows dance on silent ground,
Mystic echoes in silence found.
Under the moon's tender gaze,
We wander through night's shimmering maze.

Each breath a pause, a gentle sigh,
As time melts softly, like the sky.
Crickets serenade the velvet air,
Inviting a moment, serene and rare.

Veils of darkness embrace our fears,
Yet reveal the wonders through the years.
In the stillness, our hearts ignite,
Guided by love's ethereal light.

As dawn approaches, the veil will fade,
But the memory of night won't evade.
In the heart's chamber, it will remain,
A tapestry woven with joy and pain.

Frosted Dreams of the Universe

In the stillness of winter's breath,
Frosted dreams dance, embracing death.
The cosmos blankets in crystal white,
Illuminating shadows, a delicate sight.

Stars flicker like frost on leaves,
Whispers of magic the night believes.
Each twinkle a promise, each shimmer a chance,
Inviting our souls to a distant dance.

The universe sighs with quiet grace,
While the frost paints its lingering lace.
In the chill of night, warmth can be found,
In the embrace of love, hearts unbound.

Cold winds carry secrets untold,
Of galaxies spinning, of dreams bold.
With each breath, we touch the divine,
In this frosted dream, your hand in mine.

As we wander through starlit trails,
The universe sings in whispered scales.
In the frosted shimmer, we seek and roam,
Finding solace, together, at home.

The Quietude of Night

Night blankets the earth in soothing embrace,
Stars shine softly, each in its place.
The world whispers secrets in muted tone,
In the quietude, we feel less alone.

The moonlight dances on rippling streams,
Casting reflections of forgotten dreams.
In gentle silence, the heart reflects,
Finding solace where the soul connects.

Beneath the vast and tranquil sky,
Our worries fade, like clouds drifting by.
With every star, a wish takes flight,
Carried on wings of the coming night.

As shadows blend with a darkened hue,
We breathe in peace as the world renews.
Crickets sing soft lullabies so clear,
In this quiet place, we hold what's dear.

So let the night wrap you in its calm,
Embrace the stillness, let it be a balm.
For in the quietude, love shines bright,
Guiding us gently through the dark night.

Silvered Shadows on Frosted Ground

Silver shadows stretch so wide,
They dance upon the chilled earth.
Beneath the moon's soft, tender side,
Whispers of frost bring their mirth.

The trees, they shimmer, bright and bare,
Encased in glistening ice.
A tranquil hush fills the cool air,
Nature's beauty, a precise slice.

Footsteps crunch on sparkling trails,
Each sound a soft caress,
The world on a canvas of pale scales,
Winter's art, a gentle dress.

Stars twinkle in the frosty sky,
Reflecting light on frozen streams.
Time seems to pause, and I sigh,
Caught in this land of dreams.

In silvered shadows, solace found,
As night embraces all around.

Whispers of the Winter Night

Whispers float upon the breeze,
As winter wraps the world in white.
Beneath the trees, the shadows tease,
Embracing stillness of the night.

Glistening flakes fall from the sky,
Each one a star, a silent prayer.
Together they weave, as time flows by,
In this serene, enchanted air.

Moonlight bathes the snowy ground,
Creating realms of dreams untold.
A canvas where beauty can be found,
In silver and blue, a sight to behold.

The world sleeps in a soft embrace,
Wrapped in winter's gentle sigh.
Every flake finds its perfect place,
Under the vast, endless sky.

In whispers of this wintry night,
Hope glimmers, warm and bright.

Celestial Frost

Under the gaze of celestial frost,
The earth transforms in quiet grace.
Each breath a cloud, in moments lost,
Nature wears its winter face.

Stars drip light on frosted trees,
A tapestry of gleaming hues.
The wind carries secrets in the breeze,
A melody that softly ensues.

Crystals form on branches high,
Glistening in the moon's embrace.
An icy chorus fills the sky,
While shadows dance in their place.

Every flake a wish, a dream,
Carried on the winds of fate.
In this realm, magic seems to gleam,
As time slows, and hearts await.

Celestial frost, a gentle call,
In winter's arms, we find our all.

Glistening Dreams in the Dark

In the dark, where silence reigns,
Glistening dreams begin to rise.
Whispers of magic hold no chains,
As shadows play beneath the skies.

Glittering stars blink softly here,
Casting wishes on the ground.
The night air hums, so calm and clear,
In this serenity, we're found.

Each breath of frost wraps us tight,
Cradling hopes within its chill.
Glistening dreams take fragile flight,
Painting visions, old and still.

In every shimmer, stories weave,
Moments caught in a fleeting glance.
Believe, dear heart, and soon you'll see,
The magic within this dance.

Glistening dreams in the dark, reside,
In every heart, they confide.

Hushed Echoes Under the Sky

Whispers float upon the breeze,
Gentle songs of twilight's ease.
Stars above begin to glow,
Painting dreams in softest flow.

Moonlit shadows stretch and sway,
In the quiet, night holds sway.
Every heartbeat, every sigh,
Murmurs dance with clouds on high.

Beneath the veil of endless night,
Silence wraps the world so tight.
Echoes of the day now fade,
Peaceful thoughts in starlight laid.

Chasing secrets of the deep,
While the heavens softly weep.
Hushed reflections fill the air,
In this moment, none compare.

Time stands still, a fleeting spark,
In the canvas of the dark.
Each breath carries hope anew,
Hushed echoes call, as dreams come true.

Chill of Distant Galaxies

Cold winds flow from starry realms,
Whispers of forgotten helms.
Nebulae in swirling dance,
Invite the mind to take a chance.

Frigid light from ages past,
Brushes hearts with shadows cast.
In the void, a silence grows,
As time weaves through cosmic flows.

Galaxies in endless flight,
Painting skies with specks of light.
Each glimmer tells a tale untold,
Of ancient worlds and dreams of old.

Cloaked in dreams of starlit skies,
The chill reveals where beauty lies.
In the vastness, hope endures,
As the cosmos still assures.

Through the darkness, visions spark,
Of the wonders of the dark.
Chill of space surrounds us all,
Yet within our hearts, we call.

Frosted Tranquility

In a world of ice and snow,
Tranquil beauty starts to grow.
Every flake, a whispered prayer,
Hangs in silence, crisp and rare.

Moonlight kisses frozen streams,
Crafting silver, woven dreams.
Nature rests, its breath so light,
Wrapped in frosted cloaks of white.

Beneath the trees, the shadows play,
Winter's chill holds night at bay.
Gentle echoes, soft and sweet,
In the hush, our souls can meet.

Frosted branches softly sway,
Guiding thoughts to drift away.
In the stillness, warmth ignites,
A peaceful heart in winter's nights.

Crystals shimmer, stars align,
As the night begins to shine.
Embracing all the quiet grace,
Frosted tranquility, our space.

Silent Serenade of the Stars

A symphony of twinkling lights,
Whispers in the velvet nights.
Stars together softly hum,
In the dark, a sweetened thrum.

Each note dances through the air,
Bringing peace beyond compare.
The universe, an endless song,
Where we feel we all belong.

Gentle rhythms touch the soul,
Carried on the night's soft roll.
Filling dreams with cosmic grace,
As we drift in starry space.

Melodies of ancient time,
Guide us through this life's sweet rhyme.
In silent serenades we find,
Connections of the heart and mind.

So let the heavens sing aloud,
Wrapping us in silver shroud.
Silent beats in twilight's embrace,
A serenade, our sacred place.

Embrace of the Icy Galaxy

In the stillness of the night,
Stars flicker, diamonds bright.
A cosmic dance of cold and light,
An embrace in endless flight.

Galactic winds whisper dreams,
Carving paths through frozen beams.
Echoes of timeless schemes,
Holding onto the quiet themes.

The moon wraps all in silver hue,
Each shadow blends with the blue.
A tranquil heart waits for you,
In this universe so true.

Nebulas swirl in muted grace,
Each star a story to trace.
Lost within this endless space,
We find our timeless place.

Crystals gleam in the void's weave,
Where hope and wonder believe.
In icy realms, we retrieve,
A love that helps us cleave.

Chilled Serenade

A whispered note on winter's breath,
A chilled serenade, life and death.
Frosted echoes, nature's wreath,
In every flake, a moment's depth.

The trees are cloaked in crystal white,
Sway gently in the fading light.
A song so sweet, yet full of fright,
As shadows play through a frosty night.

Underneath a blanket cold,
The stories of the stars unfold.
In this silence, secrets told,
Of dreams within the bitter hold.

The night reveals a hidden spark,
In darkness comes a shining mark.
A serenade, crisp and stark,
Guides us through until it's dark.

With every note that cuts the air,
A promise lingers, sweet and rare.
In this chill, our hearts laid bare,
Together, we shall always share.

Glistening Nightfall

As twilight yawns and sun sinks low,
A glistening dance begins to grow.
Stars awaken with a gentle glow,
The world adorned in silver snow.

Each sparkle whispers soft and clear,
A silent hymn for all to hear.
In nightfall's arms, we cast aside fear,
Embraced by wonders, ever near.

Frosted meadows call our names,
Draped in beauty that never tames.
A sparkling realm without blames,
Where dreams take flight and love inflames.

The air is crisp, a magic thread,
We follow trails where angels tread.
In dusk's embrace, our hearts are wed,
In glistening nightfall, joy is spread.

Underneath the vast expanse,
We twirl and leap in frozen dance.
With each moment, we take a chance,
In glimmering hope, we find romance.

Frost-Laden Horizons

Beyond the hills, where frost takes hold,
Horizons gleam, a tale untold.
Wrapped in wonder, soft and bold,
The beauty of the chill unfolds.

Morning breaks with icy breath,
Awakens life, whispers of death.
An endless hush, a quiet depth,
As nature sings her frozen test.

With every step on crisp white ground,
The world around wraps dreams profound.
In silent awe, our hearts are bound,
While frost-laden whispers spin around.

The sun emerges, a gentle kiss,
Transforming ice to sparkling bliss.
In this realm, we find our wish,
As moments meet in twilight's mist.

Across horizons, hope takes flight,
In synchrony, we face the night.
With every chill, a sheer delight,
Frost-laden dreams our hearts ignite.

Radiant Ice

Crystals dance upon the lake,
Reflecting hues of morning's wake.
Whispers of the winter chill,
Nature's silence, pure and still.

A frosty breath, a soft embrace,
Each flake adorned with delicate grace.
Sunlight kisses icy ground,
In this calm, pure peace is found.

Frozen rivers gently gleam,
Carving paths like nature's dream.
A world transformed, vast and bright,
In the glow of winter's light.

Time slows down, a gentle pause,
Underneath this frosted cause.
Moments linger, soft and sweet,
Where silence and the cold hearts meet.

And as the twilight draws near,
Soft shadows start to appear.
In the stillness, winter sings,
The beauty in the cold it brings.

A Galactic Winter Serenade

Stars above like diamonds glow,
In the night, the cold winds blow.
Galactic whispers, cosmic breeze,
Drifting softly through the trees.

Nebulas in shades so bright,
Painting darkness with pure light.
Each celestial body spins,
As the tranquil serenade begins.

Among the frozen twilight skies,
Dreams of starlight softly rise.
Harmonies of silence play,
In this vast, enchanting sway.

Echoes of the universe,
A melody immersed in verse.
Snowflakes dance with cosmic grace,
This winter song, a warm embrace.

With every glimmering note we find,
The secrets of the night unwind.
A cosmic tune, forever bright,
A winter serenade of light.

Serenade Among Celestial Bodies

In the silence of the night,
Planets twirl in gentle flight.
Moons and stars in rhythm sway,
A cosmic dance, a soft ballet.

Galaxies whisper to the cold,
Ancient stories yet untold.
Gravity's pull, a silent guide,
In this vastness, we abide.

Orbits trace the timeless path,
Creating harmony and math.
Each twinkle holds a tune so pure,
The universe sings, love's allure.

Through the vastness, dreams ignite,
Sparks of wonder, sheer delight.
As we gaze at skies so grand,
Connected, we together stand.

In this serenade's embrace,
We find peace in time and space.
Among celestial bodies, we roam,
In the starlit night, we're home.

Starlit Coolness

Cool night air, a crisp delight,
Stars above, a twinkling sight.
Moonlight bathes the world in grace,
A tranquil stillness we embrace.

Beneath the sky's vast, endless dome,
Hearts alight, we feel at home.
Whispers of the cool night breeze,
Swaying gently through the trees.

Each shining orb a wishful glance,
In the quiet, we find romance.
The universe, a beckoning call,
In this stillness, we stand tall.

With every breath, the night expands,
Boundless dreams slip through our hands.
Together in this starry night,
We chase the echoes of the light.

In frosty moments, love is found,
Starlit coolness wraps around.
To the rhythm of the night we sway,
Lost in wonder till the day.

Twilight's Whisper

The sun dips low, a soft goodbye,
Shadows stretch across the sky.
Whispers of dusk in colors blend,
Night unfolds, as day must end.

Stars awaken in the deepening hue,
Casting dreams where hopes ensue.
Crickets sing their evening tune,
Underneath the watchful moon.

Gentle breezes start to sway,
Carrying scents of fading day.
In twilight's calm, the world stands still,
Embracing night's enchanting thrill.

The horizon wears a velvet coat,
As the last light begins to float.
Clouds arrayed in purple haze,
Mark the transition of daylight's phase.

In every corner, shadows creep,
As nature drifts into her sleep.
Twilight whispers secrets old,
In hushed tones, the night unfolds.

Frosted Starlight

In silent woods, the frost does gleam,
Beneath the stars, a silver dream.
Each leaf glistens, each branch a sight,
Bathed in the glow of frosted light.

Whispers float on chilly air,
Magic lingers everywhere.
The night wraps all in crystal grace,
A tranquil hush, an endless space.

Footsteps muffled by the frost,
In this quiet, we are lost.
Petals edged with icy dew,
Nature's art in shimmering view.

Moonlight spills a gentle scheme,
Reflecting on the world's sweet dream.
Frosted starlight, calm and bright,
Guiding souls through winter's night.

As stars twinkle in the dark,
Each one a magic, tiny spark.
Under this vast celestial dome,
The heart finds solace, a true home.

Beneath Celestial Glimmers

Underneath the vast expanse,
Stars ignite in cosmic dance.
The night unfolds, a sacred sight,
Whispers travel through the night.

Galaxies spin with time's embrace,
In this dark, our dreams find space.
Comets blaze their fleeting trails,
Telling stories through the gales.

Moonbeams cast a gentle glow,
Lighting paths we long to know.
Every shimmer speaks to hearts,
Binding souls, as light departs.

Winds of night begin to sigh,
Secrets shared in the starry sky.
In this realm of cosmic light,
We lay our burdens, free from fright.

Beneath celestial glimmers bright,
Hope ignites in sacred night.
Every wish upon a star,
Takes our spirit very far.

The Night's Icy Breath

The world is hushed; it holds its breath,
Touched by winter's kiss of death.
Between the trees, a chill does creep,
As shadows fall, the earth's asleep.

Frosted whispers, sharp and clear,
Echo softly, drawing near.
The moon hangs low, a glowing sphere,
Watching over all we hold dear.

In this stillness, time will pause,
Wrapped in nature's frozen laws.
Stars align in the silent void,
Gifts of night that can't be destroyed.

The icy breath of night surrounds,
As peace descends on sleeping grounds.
Dreams take flight in the wintry air,
Floating softly, without a care.

Amidst the frost, our hearts beat strong,
In the night, where we belong.
The icy breath whispers low,
Of stories only night can know.

Glowing Frost Under Moonlight

A whisper sweeps through silent glades,
The moonlight dances, casting shades.
Frosty crystals sparkle bright,
Glimmers twinkle in the night.

Trees adorned with silver lace,
Nature's beauty, a timeless grace.
Footsteps crunch on icy ground,
In this magic, peace is found.

Stars peek through the velvet sky,
In the stillness, dreams can fly.
Every breath, a cloud of mist,
Moments like this can't be missed.

Whispers linger among the pines,
As the world in slumber shines.
Frosty air, a chill so sweet,
At this hour, life feels complete.

Moonlit paths where shadows play,
Guiding hearts along the way.
In the chill of winter's night,
Frosty magic feels so right.

Perpetual Night's Embrace

In shadows deep where secrets dwell,
A story spun, a silent spell.
Endless twilight wraps the land,
In its grip, we softly stand.

Stars above in cosmic dance,
Echo dreams of ancient chance.
Moonbeams kiss the darkened earth,
A cradle for the night's rebirth.

Whispers of the creeping fog,
Embrace the world like a gentle cog.
Softly drifting on the breeze,
Time suspends, as moments freeze.

Each heartbeat echoes through the dark,
Guided by an unseen spark.
Perpetual night, a friend so near,
Cradling dreams, calming fear.

With every sigh, the stars align,
In this realm, your heart is mine.
Embrace the stillness, find the light,
In this eternal, sacred night.

Cosmic Drift in the Frost

In the stillness of the night,
Celestial bodies shine so bright.
Frosty flakes like stardust fall,
Whispers of the universe call.

Galaxies spin in silent grace,
As we drift through time and space.
Cosmic wonders hold us near,
In this cold, there's nothing to fear.

The Milky Way, a river of light,
Guides our dreams in frosty flight.
Echoes of hearts in the void,
Sacred moments, never destroyed.

In this vast, unyielding air,
We find our solace, strong and rare.
Cosmic drift, forever binds,
In frosty whispers, love unwinds.

Planets dance in harmony,
Tales untold of you and me.
Under stars, we weave our fate,
In the frost, we linger late.

Shivering Glimmers

The dawn breaks soft with chilly breath,
Whispers of dawn from twilight's depth.
Shivering glimmers, a fragile sight,
Waking dreams in morning light.

Nature shivers, breathes anew,
Each twinkle dances, sparkling dew.
Colors bloom in golden hues,
As night retreats, the world renews.

In the crisp air, a promise gleams,
Chasing shadows, chasing dreams.
Heartbeats quicken in the glow,
With each pulse, the warmth does flow.

Endless wonders lie in wait,
In every corner, every fate.
Shivering glimmers of the dawn,
Awaken softly, the world drawn.

With each hour, the day expands,
Painting beauty with gentle hands.
In the light, we find our bliss,
Moments cherished, not to miss.

Sparkling Nighttime Secrets

Stars twinkle high in the sky,
Whispers of dreams gently fly.
Moonlight dances on fresh dew,
Secrets of night, known to few.

Shadows play in silvery streams,
Wrapped in the warmth of soft dreams.
Cool breeze carries the night's song,
In this moment, where we belong.

The world sleeps beneath a blanket,
In calm quiet, hearts do bank it.
Mysteries call, softly they hum,
In the night, we become one.

Every flicker ignites the past,
Moments in light, forever cast.
Sparkling truths in midnight's sight,
Guardians of tales, pure and bright.

As dawn approaches, stars will fade,
Yet in our hearts, dreams are laid.
In sparkling whispers, we'll confide,
Nighttime secrets forever reside.

Frigid Fantasies

Chill of the air, crisp and clear,
Winter's enchantment, drawing near.
In frost-laden fields, dreams unfurl,
Frigid fantasies begin to swirl.

Whispers of snowflakes kiss the ground,
Silent beauty in silence found.
Each crystal a wish, pure and bright,
Frigid fantasies ignite the night.

Beneath the glow of a frosty moon,
Hearts are warm in winter's tune.
Wrapped in blankets, tales we share,
Finding magic in the cold air.

Branches shimmer, cloaked in white,
Nature's wonders, a wondrous sight.
In the stillness, our dreams take flight,
Frigid fantasies dance in the night.

As morning breaks with golden rays,
Frigid fantasies still amaze.
In every breath, the chill persists,
In winter's grasp, we still exist.

Frostbitten Poetry

Words wrapped tightly, crisp and cold,
Frostbitten verses, stories told.
Each line a breath, sharp and pure,
In winter's grasp, thoughts are sure.

Papers shiver under icy air,
Fingers dance, crafting the rare.
Every stanza, a glistening shard,
Frostbitten poetry guards the heart.

Each letter formed with care and grace,
Delicate thoughts, in time and space.
Winter's chill drapes over the page,
Capturing moments, like a sage.

The world outside, a quiet muse,
Frozen landscapes in vibrant hues.
In the stillness, inspiration grows,
Frostbitten poetry, life bestows.

As thawing dawn approaches near,
Embers of warmth begin to clear.
Yet in the frost, we find our way,
Frostbitten poetry, here to stay.

Snowy Stardust

Gentle flakes of snow alight,
Whirling softly in the night.
Each one a wish, a cosmic spark,
Snowy stardust, bright and stark.

Blankets of cream cover the earth,
Whispers of magic, winter's worth.
Under starlit skies, we roam,
Dancing in dreams, far from home.

Every snowfall evokes a sigh,
As memories drift and glide by.
Each twinkle echoes in the cold,
Snowy stardust, tales unfold.

Footprints traced in frosty air,
Marking moments, memories rare.
In the hush of night, we find,
Snowy stardust, one of a kind.

As morning rises, shadows fade,
Yet in the sparkles, dreams are laid.
In every flake, a piece of heart,
Snowy stardust, never depart.

Gentle Breeze Beneath the Stars

The night unfolds with whispers soft,
Beneath the stars, the world lifts off.
A gentle breeze, a sweet embrace,
In this calm, we find our place.

The shadows dance with silver light,
The moon bestows its quiet might.
As dreams take flight on wings of night,
Hearts entwined, everything's right.

The trees sway gently, skies so vast,
Moments cherished, memories cast.
In whispered tales, we find our tune,
With every breath, we welcome June.

The stars above, like diamonds glow,
In every heart, a radiant show.
With hands held tight, we drift along,
To nature's hum, we weave our song.

So here we stand, mid whispers bright,
Beneath the stars, the world ignites.
With every sigh and laughter shared,
In gentle breeze, our souls are bared.

Frosted Wonderment

A morning cloak of icy breath,
Envelops all in quiet death.
Each blade of grass, a crystal knife,
In frost, we see the dance of life.

The trees adorned in shimmering white,
Stand proud and tall in morning light.
With every step, a crunch, a sound,
In this cool world, pure joy is found.

The air is crisp, a chilling kiss,
In frosted wonder, there's pure bliss.
Nature's art, a delicate lace,
In every flake, a soft embrace.

As sunlight breaks, it warms the ground,
With colors bright that soon surround.
In this moment, time stands still,
With frosted wonders, hearts we fill.

So let us wander, hand in hand,
Through this enchanted, frosty land.
For in the chill, our spirits soar,
In wonderment, we crave for more.

Celestial Calm

In twilight's hush, the world takes pause,
The stars emerge without a cause.
A peaceful heart, a gentle sigh,
In celestial calm, the spirits fly.

The heavens stretch, a velvet dome,
In silence deep, we find our home.
Each twinkle lights our hopes and dreams,
In magic's grasp, the starlight beams.

The constellations weave their tales,
Across the night, like whispered gales.
With every glance, we're drawn above,
In cosmic dance, we learn of love.

The night unfolds, inviting peace,
With every breath, our worries cease.
In quiet moments, wisdom reigns,
A tranquil mind that never wanes.

So let us bask in night's embrace,
In celestial calm, we find our grace.
For in this stillness, hearts align,
In starlit dreams, our souls entwine.

Vibrant Stars in Frost

Amidst the chill, the night ignites,
With vibrant stars, a dazzling sight.
Frosted fields like mirrors gleam,
In icy realms, we chase a dream.

The cosmos casts its glowing veil,
As winter winds begin to wail.
In this bright arc of silver light,
We find our path, our hearts take flight.

Each star a beacon, bright and bold,
In frosty air, their tales unfold.
With every breath, the night inspires,
In frozen landscapes, kindles fires.

So let us wander, hand in hand,
Through realms of frost, a mystic land.
With vibrant stars as our guide,
In their embrace, we'll learn to glide.

For in this stillness, hope won't fade,
With vibrant stars, our dreams are made.
In every glance, a wish to see,
A world aglow, forever free.

Celestial Whispers

In the dark above, stars gleam bright,
Softly they sing, a lullaby of light.
Ancient tales carried on the breeze,
Echoes of dreams beneath the trees.

Wonders unfold in the velvet sky,
As constellations weave and sigh.
A secret dance that never ends,
Where the universe's magic bends.

Each twinkle a word, each glow a thought,
In silence, the wisdom of ages sought.
Time pauses here in this sacred space,
A cosmic embrace, a timeless grace.

Galaxies whisper in cosmic streams,
Filling the night with glimmering beams.
Together we drift through the endless night,
Lost in the splendor of purest light.

With every breath, the stars align,
In the vast web of fate, we intertwine.
Celestial whispers cradle our souls,
Forever bound in this night's controls.

Icy Stars at Dawn

Silent winds carry the chill of night,
As icy stars fade with morning light.
Whispers of dreams drift into the blue,
Dawn's soft fingers brush the dew.

In the frost-kissed air, shadows dance,
Nature awakens in a quiet trance.
Each breath visible, a fleeting sigh,
As the sun rises, painting the sky.

Crystals shimmer on blades of grass,
Holding the secrets of night, they pass.
A transient moment of frozen grace,
Before warmth takes hold, in this sacred space.

Birdsongs break the serene embrace,
Bringing to life this tranquil place.
Icy stars bidding their soft goodbye,
As day unfolds in a brilliant sigh.

A new journey begins with the dawn,
Lessons learned from the night's calm drawn.
In the heart of morning, the world awakes,
As icy stars melt in sunlight's stakes.

Shivering Nightscapes

In the shadowed woods where whispers dwell,
Mysterious echoes of night's soft spell.
Silvery moonlight drapes the trees,
A world transformed, kissed by the breeze.

Each rustle a story, each sigh a song,
In this realm where the brave belong.
Stars like lanterns in the heavens bright,
Guide lost souls through the shivering night.

Fingers of fog weave through the air,
Caressing the stillness, a tender care.
The pulse of the earth is slow and deep,
In shadows we wander, our secrets to keep.

Glimmers of light dance on the stream,
Reflections echo a twilight dream.
Nightscapes whisper in softest tones,
Elder shadows, the silent stones.

As dawn approaches, the chill will wane,
Shivering nightscapes will fade again.
Memories born in the moonlit sigh,
Remain in the heart as the moments fly.

Cosmic Chill

In the void where silence reigns supreme,
A cosmic chill wraps the universe's dream.
Stars pulse gently, their glowing sighs,
In the stillness that stretches and flies.

Nebulae paint the canvas of night,
Colors blending in celestial light.
Time drifts softly like a feathered quill,
Writing the secrets of the cosmic chill.

Galaxies spin in a dance so grand,
Whirling together, hand in hand.
Each moment a heartbeat, a flickering spark,
Illuminating the endless dark.

Comets trace paths in this vast expanse,
Whispers of wonders that dare to dance.
Through the chill, we find warmth within,
In the thread of starlight where we begin.

As we gaze upwards, our spirits soar,
Embracing the chill that beckons for more.
In the cosmos wide, our hearts align,
In the embrace of infinity, we find the divine.

Silhouettes in the Moonlight

Beneath the silver glow, we stand,
Shadows cast by dreams so grand.
Whispers wrapped in night's embrace,
Time slows down, a gentle pace.

Figures swaying, soft and light,
Hearts entwined in sweet delight.
In this moment, bound we feel,
Silent vows, a love so real.

The moon a witness to our fate,
Every sigh that we create.
Here beneath the starry skies,
We find our truth, we find our ties.

With every glance, the world fades away,
In your arms, forever I'll stay.
A silhouette against the night,
Together we will chase the light.

Shivers Among the Cosmos

In the vastness, stars align,
Each a whisper, each a sign.
Galaxies spin in a dance,
Drawing dreams, igniting chance.

Shivers coursing through my soul,
As we drift, we become whole.
Nebulas swirl with colors bright,
Painting love in cosmic light.

The universe, our secret friend,
Stardust paths that never end.
Feel the gravity of your gaze,
Lost in this ethereal maze.

Eclipsed by wonders far and wide,
Here with you, I choose to glide.
Among the stars, we chase our dreams,
Flowing through celestial streams.

Glacial Dreams

Frozen whispers in the air,
Softly drifting, light as hair.
Mountains rise with icy grace,
Nature's breath, a tranquil space.

In the stillness, hearts will soar,
As we glide on winter's floor.
Crystal visions, pure and bright,
Shimmer softly in the night.

Snowflakes dance, a gentle art,
Painting dreams upon the heart.
Each a chance, a fleeting spark,
Guiding us through realms of dark.

Together, we will navigate,
Through these glacial dreams await.
Embrace the chill, the love we find,
In the frosty night, entwined.

The Quiet Dance of Stars

In the silence, stars appear,
Twinkling softly, drawing near.
A quiet dance in cosmic space,
Time and light in sweet embrace.

With every movement, shadows sway,
Gentle rhythms lead the way.
Caught in this celestial trance,
Underneath the midnight expanse.

Galaxies waltz, a timeless song,
In this wonder, we belong.
Planetary whispers guide our hearts,
Connecting voids, where love imparts.

So let the stars our secrets keep,
In silence, let our spirits leap.
With each twinkle, dreams ascend,
In the quiet, we'll transcend.

Milton Keynes UK
Ingram Content Group UK Ltd.
UKHW010232111224
452348UK00011B/687